HURRICANE

by Jessica Rudolph

Consultant:
Dr. Charles A. Doswell III
Doswell Scientific Consulting
NOAA Severe Storms Scientist (retired)

BEARPORT
PUBLISHING

New York, New York

Credits

Cover, © iStockphoto/Thinkstock; 4–5, © Danita Delimont/Alamy; 6–7, © Zacarias Pereira da Mata/Alamy; 8–9, © dpa/Corbis; 10–11, © AP Photo/David J. Phillip; 12–13, © Marko Georgiev/Getty Images; 14–15, © ERIC GAY/AP/Corbis; 16, © Chris Sattlberger/Anzenberger/Redux; 16–17, © PATRICK SCHNEIDER KRT/Newscom; 18–19, © Jose Luis Magana/AP/Corbis; 20–21, © Julie Dermansky/Corbis; 21, © Scott Houston/Corbis; 22, © dpa/Corbis; 23TL, © Dubova/Shutterstock; 23TR, © paintings/Shutterstock; 23BL, © Danita Delimont/Alamy; 23BR, © AP Photo/Alan Diaz.

Publisher: Kenn Goin
Creative Director: Spencer Brinker
Design: Debrah Kaiser
Photo Researcher: Picture Perfect Professionals, LLC

Library of Congress Cataloging-in-Publication Data in process at time of publication (2014)
Library of Congress Control Number: 2013038754
ISBN-13: 978-1-62724-127-4

For more information, write to Bearport Publishing Company, Inc., 45 West 21st Street, Suite 3B, New York, New York 10010. Printed in the United States of America.

10 9 8 7 6 5 4 3 2 1

CONTENTS

Hurricanes 4

Hurricane Facts 22

Glossary 23

Index .24

Read More 24

Learn More Online 24

About the Author 24

HURRICANES

Rain falls along the **coast**.

Trees bend from the swirling winds.

A **hurricane** is coming!

A hurricane is a giant spinning storm. It has heavy rains and strong winds.

Winds whip up the ocean water.

Crash!

Waves smash onto the beach.

Hurricanes are also called typhoons or cyclones.

Hurricanes form over the ocean.

Sometimes, they move to the coast.

On land, hurricanes are dangerous.

land

Hurricanes are huge. They can be up to 1,000 miles (1,609 km) across.

ocean

hurricane

9

A hurricane's winds knock over trees.

They blast out windows.

They blow roofs off houses!

Hurricane winds can blow more than 155 miles per hour (249 kph).

Hurricane winds push walls of ocean water onto land.

This is called a storm surge.

Hurricane rains and storm surges cause **floods.**

Storm surges can be more than 20 feet (6 m) high.

Water from floods covers streets.

Rushing water may get into homes.

Sometimes, people get trapped by the water.

Rescue workers try to save people who are trapped by floods.

Hurricanes often take days to reach land.

This gives people time to get to a safe place.

Check **weather reports** to find out if a hurricane is coming.

If a hurricane hits, stay inside.

Keep far away from windows.

Then broken glass won't hit you.

Some people board up windows before a hurricane hits. This helps keep winds and flying objects from breaking the glass.

Hurricanes often destroy homes and towns.

People work hard to rebuild them after the storm.

It can take years to fix damage caused by a hurricane.

HURRICANE FACTS

- Hurricanes spin in a circle. The center is called the eye.

- Most hurricanes that hit the United States occur in the southeastern part of the country.

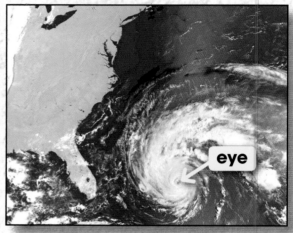

eye

- Hurricanes are given names. Some hurricanes that have hit the United States were named Andrew, Rita, and Katrina.

- Hurricane winds and storm surges can knock out power lines and electricity.

- If you live in an area where hurricanes occur, keep flashlights, blankets, bottled water, and food on hand.

GLOSSARY

coast (KOHST) land that runs along an ocean

floods (FLUHDZ) huge flows of water that spread over land

hurricane (HUR-uh-*kane*) a storm that forms in the ocean, with very high winds and heavy rain

weather reports (WETH-ur ri-PORTS) reports that tell what the weather will be like in the coming hours or days

23

INDEX

coast 4, 8
damage 10, 13, 15, 18, 21, 22
flood 13, 15
ocean 7, 8, 13

rain 4–5, 13
safety 16, 18, 22
winds 4–5, 7, 10–11, 13, 18, 22

READ MORE

Gibbons, Gail. *Hurricanes!* New York: Holiday House (2009).

Simon, Seymour. *Hurricanes*. New York: HarperCollins (2003).

LEARN MORE ONLINE

To learn more about hurricanes, visit
www.bearportpublishing.com/ItsaDisaster!

ABOUT THE AUTHOR

Jessica Rudolph lives in Connecticut. She has edited and written many books about history, science, and nature for children.